# THE DANCING LIGHT OF DAWN

#InstantEternal Poetry Vol 1

#PoetryCommunity

Copyright © 2021 Stuart Matthews & Contributors

All rights reserved

No part of this book may be reproduced, or stored in a retrieval system, or transmitted in any form or by any means, electronic, mechanical, photocopying, recording, or otherwise, without express written permission of the publisher.

# INTRODUCTION

#InstantEternal is a poetry prompt on Twitter, giving writers inspiration to create their own piececes of work. This poetry book would not have been possible without the wonderful contributions from the Twitter poetry community. They have really done a fabulous job at using the prompts, to create such a wonderful book. A huge thank you to the following contributors -

@atreya2112, @Bliss_Missed, @AudreySemprun, @21composed, @Ainneamhag, @QueenofCups99, @JayHeltzer, @Mjustthat, @DKMarieAuthor, @Catkin1973, @sweetdarkpoetry, @bionicanadian, @hubner_t, @smusicj68, @kaleidopathic, @MadQueenStorm, @JessicaELaymon, @relaroca, @hsdee, @pallavi31, @antsared, @BklynMercado, @LairdOfTheHeart, @CattyKoala, @AstolaJalpari, @femfict, @parkini422, @OMANXL1, @dark_backup, @UKavyajanani, @Free2bmac, @AmandaJK_, @annieb222, @HangryPoet197, @JamSt1977, @Silentecho64, @ThePuckishPen, @DanielC55186873, @lightm0tifs, @SerlinaRose767, @jillwebbwords, @ViewfinderPM, @BithiPaulAuthor, @alternativepen, @Story_Tweets, @WhimsyCheshire, @katy_lady_b, @AmellMirai, @CMamathi, @BenjaminDStone, @RainyDayRibbons, @livezformusic, @mssakshinarula, @Lilly2Rose3, @FortunatusL, @eharperpoetry

# PROMPTS

All the contributors took inspiration from the following #InstantEternal poetry prompts, whether used in their entirity, or partially -

The Dancing Light Of Dawn
In Meadows Abloom
A Whispered Summer's Haze
Dripping Sunlight
Crystal Shimmered Waters
The Glistening Ocean's Call
Tapestry Of Flowers
Beneath A Midnight Chandelier Of Stars
Welcomed Summer Rain
A Mosaic Of Dreams
Within Cascades Of Starlight
As Morning Kisses The Sky
As Diamonds Dance In The Flow
A Summer's Season Of Love
The Breath Of Midnight Warmth

# POEM 1

Lunar eyes of existence
That are olden,
The dancing light of Dawn
Bestows enchantment
Of the soul~
How sweet immortal fires
Of night
Are golden,
For the solstice of the summer,
~
Till the darkening
Of the cold..

Poem by - Dawn Serbert @atreya2112

# POEM 2

In meadows abloom with wildflowers,
I pick them from my heart,
tied in satin string,
holds my everything.
In the dancing light of dawn,
carving words to love upon,
pressed in pages of my favorite book,
I trace every line
each time I look
sated, shook.

Poem by - Bliss @Bliss_Missed

# POEM 3

The dancing light of dawn
obscured by the faint sparkle of the silvery moon
Tomorrows hopes and dreams
shadowed by yesterdays pain
Yet hope prevails in meadows abloom
with a love that will never die
The scent of roses fill the air
And only dreams survive

Poem by - iAmWriting @AudreySemprun

# POEM 4

Holding hands
a promise kept
we tiptoe silently
on dew moistened blades
Oh lush verdant dawn reveal
to penitent lovers
in striated splendour
our pastures new
Greener were indeed the meadows beyond
As the last of the dying petals fall
new blooms present

Poem by - COMPOSED @21composed

# POEM 5

Through the dancing
Light of dawn
Your horizon awaits
Calling you to embrace
Immerse
In the heat
Of this
Instant
Eternal love

Poem by - Grace @Ainneamhag

# POEM 6

Meadows abloom
awash in the dancing light of Summer dawn
Ballet of breeze and wildflowers
Pink Lady's Slipper Pirouette
Paintbrush plies
Tender touch
the warm, soft kiss of morn

Poem by - Merry Maiden @QueenofCups99

# POEM 7

### Conflict

Bedsheet warmth
and cooled oscillated bedroom air
mix their messages against summer's inviting dancing
light of dawn.

Comfort's in here.
Life's out there.
You win. Embrace me, rays of sunshine, all the day long.

Poem by - Jay Heltzer - Writer @JayHeltzer

# POEM 8

The dancing light of dawn
In meadows of bloom
Sweet scented rose
Petals soft
You walk in shades of umber

Gentle caressing winds
Upon the mantle of life
Your kiss awakens
Blue skies & rainbows

A flight of doves
White wings amidst the blue

Poem by - Just M... @Mjustthat

# POEM 9

Under the fading stars
In the dancing light of dawn
You'll find her
In your retreating dreams
Swimming in a sea of possibilities
Or laying in a meadow abloom
With your fantasies

Poem by - DK Marie Romance Author @DKMarieAuthor

# POEM 10

The gentle touch of morning sun,
breathes soft light to meadows abloom.
A kiss of love shared by two,
as a flutter of butterfly wings begin.
Once lost, souls apart,
they cling to its heartbeat forever.
Knowing time may still be brief,
love falters never

Poem by - Cat @Catkin1973

# POEM 11

The time I take
To listen to the echoes
Of our past comforts me
It whispers in summer's haze
Keeping me warm
While you're no longer able
I see your smile
In the dripping sunlight
Allowing me to see
A future without you
Knowing you are
In the comforting breeze
Of my memories

Poem by - DK Marie Romance Author @DKMarieAuthor

# POEM 12

Dancing light of dawn
shoreline of painted light
my eyes daffodil in meadows abloom
birds candle branches by the blue brook shade
summer sky rolls up over hills of green
petals away the night, casts her rays
a plumage of feathers cresting
myriad of... emotions

Poem by - Kimberly @bionicanadian

# POEM 13

The dancing light of dawn
bespeckle eyes that wistfully gaze upon the morn
and heard on whispered breath
a sigh, a death
as multitudinous souls breeze by
This meadow may have gained a bloom
but a life was taken far too soon

Poem by - COMPOSED @21composed

# POEM 14

My heart seeks
a serene beat
Amongst Mother
Nature's treat
Which is the dancing
light of dawn
Upon those gardens
of ancient Babylon
Where lazy summer
days of the past
Reflect within the
still waters cast
New seasonal birth
of all things life
Upon our earth

Poem by - T.J. Hübner Writing - Poet & Author @hubner_t

# POEM 15

Refreshing lemonade by the pool
Frizzy hair decorated with jewels
Floating away to the land of make believe
Sky above clear, calm, and blue
Reflecting its light with a million clues
Tapestry of flowers and trees covered
Lay underneath for a pampered summer

Poem by - Sangeeta @smusicj68

# POEM 16

In the dancing light of dawn
new leaves shimmer
a rebirth of inner growth
hope extends a gift
of another exquisite morn

Silent are her petals
in meadows abloom
her colors speak fluently
in Mother Nature's tongue
Flora eternal perennial
I can count on thee

Poem by - kaleidopathic @kaleidopathic

# POEM 17

fox in the meadows abloom
crows in the oaks
the dancing light of dawn
shining on where the crossroads meet
follow the cottonwoods
down to the creek
listen as the morning begins to sing
summer's chorus of wind and wildflowers
a sweet greeting to awaken to

Poem by - Storm @MadQueenStorm

# POEM 18

a whispered summer haze
dripping sunlight
in a golden glaze
as the world lies drowsing
in the perfumed sighs
of honeysuckle melodies
and the warm embrace
of bluebell skies

Poem by - Storm @MadQueenStorm

# POEM 19

She was a fool for romance
A whispered summer's haze
Fogged her vision
& blurred her mind
From the overt, to the sublime
& oh, the sound of poetry
The cadence of a melody
Echoed in a warm summer breeze
Seduced by dripping sunlight
& by gentle words

Poem by - iAmWriting @AudreySemprun

# POEM 20

A whispered summer haze
heavy in the air, it hung
dripping sunlight blurring
gauze filled skies
how do I see my lilac season
of backyard pool days
having to forage through hedges
for things just out of my reach
crescent flecks of coral burning
..daylight hours

Poem by - Kimberly @bionicanadian

# POEM 21

Dripping sunlight cascades
through glass stained ajar allowing flaccid fabric
momentarily to billow
whilst summer scented breeze tease the finer tendrils
of hair that sway and are golden to the touch
Beautiful in repose you rest..
if only…

Poem by - COMPOSED @21composed

# POEM 22

Flashes sparkle as she shakes
Her glossy coat, droplets
Cascading, bits of sunlight
Sticking to our skin,
Radiate against the light.
After she licks our faces
Of dripping stars,
She chases the sprinkler,
And the cats,
With equal abandon.

Poem by - Jessica Laymon @JessicaELaymon

# POEM 23

A Whispered Summer's Haze
Nesting into my darker gaze;
Dripping Sunlight through my face
At each passing of the days.
Soon I gather your plays, prays,
And follow the rest
Into the cemetery maze;
With roses and candle trays,
I remain here, into your silence,
From May to May.

Poem by Lara Reis| Poetry @relaroca

# POEM 24

A whispered summer's haze
sensual rays caress ocean waves
dripping sunlight's adieu
sun dips into nighttime's lure
to make passionate love to the dark

Millions of heart strings
tethered to Luna's golden crescent
rock in synchrony
to rhythms of gentle waves

Poem by - kaleidopathic @kaleidopathic

# POEM 25

All my life
could be described
as a mosaic of dreams
so carefully built

An infinity of colors,
shades and shapes
yet missing that final piece
to make it complete

Poem by - Anne @sweetdarkpoetry

# POEM 26

(Symbiotic Coalescence)

Beneath dripping sunlight
Can be found a pure delight
The life force amassed
Of present and past
From death grows rebirth
Upon green pastures of earth
In meadows abloom
Is found an exquisite perfume
Those flowered scents
That summer presents
Attracting the birds and bees
Who float on the heated breeze
Amongst a colourful array
Of Mother Nature's bouquet
Signalling a freshness anew
Bidding winter and spring adieu
Creating a pallet and essence
Of unique symbiotic coalescence

Poem by - T.J. Hübner Writing - Poet & Author @hubner_t

# POEM 27

it was
an early morn
drenched
in a whispering
summer's haze
when the truth
came over me
as clear & beautiful
to my eyes
as the tangles
in her hair
& the smile she gave
our love
had become
the sea
& the stars
the giver of life
& the light that guides

Poem by - Dee Lusk @hsdee

# POEM 28

Unusual to the wind
I am
Endless,
Like a whispered summer's
Haze,
Written in the rhythm
Of the sand~
Of the grey sewn
In the blue
That leaves me breathless,
I flutter
With the butterflies,
Perfectly
Unspoken,
~
In his hand…

Poem by - Dawn Serbert @atreya2112

# POEM 29

Upon a whispered summer haze
I am carried back to childhood days
Of car journey's and seaside trips
hand in hand with mam and dad
On promenade walks
followed by fish and chips
Then out of nowhere comes the
tears, which are happy and sad
For the memories
fill my heart with glee
Knowing my mind does
still recall and see
Those magnificent
times of adolescence
Where life always was
and will be my quintessence
That joyful place of remembrance
I can revisit and imagine
When my soul sorely needs a
timeless little distraction

Poem by - T.J. Hübner Writing - Poet & Author @hubner_t

# POEM 30

as a clawing feeling
grows in her guts
the ghost of a
fading past running
familiar fingers
down her spine,
she seeks the
dancing light of dawn
for answers and closures,
promised in the
meadows abloom
sometimes with her
head below water
other times with
head above the clouds

Poem by - Pallavi @pallavi31

# POEM 31

What did you say?
Walk an extra mile?
Hardly possible!
Some days take incredible strength
Riding upon a whispered summer's haze
Cherishing the dipping sun
Just halt the sprint
Feel the breezy shore
Count your blessings, thank the Lord
Prepare for another day

Poem by - Sangeeta @smusicj68

# POEM 32

A whispered
Summers haze,
Waves upon a
Feathered breeze,
Dripping sunlight days,
Of ambience, restful Sea..

Poem by - Anthony Rhead @antsared

# POEM 33 AND 34

As I slowly open my eyes,
I see the dancing light of dawn
flashing delicious memories
of last night's summer love

~

In my daydream
you and I peacefully lie
beneath the dripping sunlight,
tanning our skin,
making you mine.

Poems by - Anne @sweetdarkpoetry

# POEM 35

Time moves on
Still memory lingers long

As i sit here sipping my tea
The cool afternoon shade
By the apple blossom tree

My eyes close momentarily
To a whispered summer's haze

To dandelion wishes
Floating in the breeze

Dripping sunlight & still your kiss

Poem by - Just M... @Mjustthat

# POEM 36 AND 37

A whispered summers haze
The beginnings of a love maze
A labyrinth of twists to solve
For our love to fully evolve

~

She welcomed summer rain
To wash away her pain
Drowning her demons
Without need or reason
His love is all that remains

Poems by - Grace @Ainneamhag

# POEM 38

Dripping sunlight
of ethereal sentient
coveting the colours of
Lathyrus odoratus
sweet pea Aegean love petals
gentler than wishes
sweeter than the scent
of a kiss in twighlights magic

Poem by - Rob Taylor @LairdOfTheHeart

# POEM 39

Walkabout dreamtime
Following ancestral ways.
Legends of the land.
Billabongs dripping sunlight,
Slipping the spring from my tears.

I whisper secrets,
Listening for ancient reply,
Dewdrops from mourning.
One song in the sisterhood.
A chorus for the dawn.

Poem by - Denise Carruthers @CattyKoala

# POEM 40

Summer Love

The devil caught your eye,
After he watched you die.
A deal of immortality,
Sealed your fatality,
A bribe of decadence,
Traitors of providence.
Dripping sunlight.
Celestial flight,
First love's summerlight
Fated firelight.

Poem by - The Mermaid of Astola Island @AstolaJalpari

# POEM 41

He held me as the rain fell,
dripping sunlight cast from summer skies.
The sweet smell of earth and leaves
as we stood beneath those ancient trees.
And I could not remember the day or hour as it passed,
but that moment was a feeling I'd hold to my last.

Poem by - Cat @Catkin1973

# POEM 42

A whispered summer's haze,
casts its tender touch upon her.
Auburn are the wisps that tease,
the sun warmed beauty of snow white skin.
The scent of her remembered,
like a jewelled garden as petals fall.
Her eyes soft they welcome him,
back where he belongs.

Poem by - Cat @Catkin1973

# POEM 43

He's
A Whispered
Summer's Haze

a hot, passionate
yet quiet
Sweat in his Heat

But impairing
All vision
To see through
his seductive
shroud that
Hung too heavy
in the air

My Eyes could
Never filter it
& my lungs
Were unable to
Ever breathe it
All in

Poem by - @femfict

# POEM 44

The end of the afternoon
At that certain point
When in the hot day
A country scene
Once dripping Sunlight
Begins to dry into the
green shoots of dusk
Quietly you perceive
The shadows lengthen
As just above the horizon
appears the Moon

Poem by - Ian Parkin @parkini422

# POEM 45

The glistening ocean's call,
the edge of sand and sea,
like a bright tapestry of flowers,
the hues call to me.
Crystal shimmered waters,
to roaring, crashing waves,
tidal pull,
fills my heart full,
as we're meant to be.

Poem by - Bliss@Bliss_Missed

# POEM 46

Crystal shimmering waters
glistening upon the ocean's call
reflections of the moon,
dusts... rippling waves
sweet-light sun sleeps in
heaven's nightdreams
until the last glimmer of night-set
vanishes into daydreams...

Poem by - Kimberly @bionicanadian

# POEM 47

Tapestry of flowers
holds the thin veil of Summer
Gossamer gift
edged in dewdrops and laced sunlight
Dawn's kiss falls sweet
upon her lips
in chiffon daydreams
that wait only
for dark velvet nights

Poem by - Merry Maiden @QueenofCups99

# POEM 48

a tapestry of flowers
colors threading among
a green warp and weft
gently spread
under a dreaming sky
stories both
ephemeral and beauteous
fragrant in their verses
shy-wild yet fiercely told

Poem by - Storm @MadQueenStorm

# POEM 49

By the crystal shimmered waters
The breeze of rainbows sunbeams

Sweet the smelling air
of salted summer

Her perfume a tapestry of flowers
An array of colour fusion
Dancing in the light

Of the glistening ocean's call
Lovers are we in waves sublime

Poem by - Just M... @Mjustthat

# POEM 50

The glistening ocean's call
Calling me to my home
Crystal shimmered waters
Beckon me once again
A hypnotic depth
Of fathoms I cannot perceive
Calling me. Yes, calling me
Waves seductive and free
In a tapestry of flowers
Bury me in the sea

Poem by - iAmWriting @AudreySemprun

# POEM 51

West Coasting! Catch me on the Pacific Coast Highway!

Answering the glistening ocean's call prompt / right away!

Enjoying the sunsets, dreams answered this stanza!

Oasis enjoyed! East Coast? back to reality I'm deployed, it's over!

Poem by - OMANXL1 @OMANXL1

# POEM 52

Surrounded by
A tapestry of flowers
Dipping her toes
Into crystal shimmered waters
The glistening ocean's call
She was at rest at the sea
She was where
She wanted to be
She had found
Tranquility
And a peace
That would never leave

Poem by - iAmWriting @AudreySemprun

# POEM 53

Dripping sunlight splatters the hot
windowsill in the
late morning
Tiny plant, I must
protect you from
it's overwhelming
rays of benevolence

Poem by - Dark Wolf Writer II More Tales to Tell @dark_backup

# POEM 54, 55 AND 56

A whispered summer's
haze fades the blue of mountains
on the distant plain

~

Welcomed summer rains
bring perfect mud for little
hands to make good pies

~

As morning kisses
the sky, I sip my warm tea
and give thanks for all

Poems by - Dark Wolf Writer II More Tales to Tell @dark_backup

# POEM 57

Your voice to her will be always
As crystal shimmered waters;
A Glistening Ocean's Call
For your granddaughter.
While you shared
With her your small hours,
Weaving a tapestry of flowers,
Baking bread, cooking meals.
You brought so much Summer,
Which now devours our encounters.

Poem by - Lara Reis | Poetry @relaroca

# POEM 58

### Silent Shore

Braid my dreams to your soul,
With the glistening ocean's call.
Crystal diamonds shimmer sail,
Waves to your silent shores prevail.
Tapestries of flowers,
Guards your secrets
Of love's sweet powers
In bittersweet regrets.

Poem by - The Mermaid of Astola Island @AstolaJalpari

# POEM 59

Stuffed with heartbreaks,
my amorphous verses
Search for a home in your
Frivolous heart.

With rues in my veins,
I splash on this
Crystal shimmered waters,
craving for a shore to
Beach this unexplainable love.

I have imbued the hue of
Daffodils.
I'm not afraid to ache.

Poem by - Kavya Janani. U @UKavyajanani

# POEM 60

the time I take
walking my tired feet
into playful crystal shimmered
waters of the warm evening sea
waves upon waves of exhaustion
gently quietened by the glistening
ocean's call as moonbeams
knowingly weave a happy
tapestry of flowers smoking in me
essence of serenity sought

Poem by - Pallavi @pallavi31

# POEM 61

Weave me in a tapestry of flowers,
let each thread bind my soul with thine.
Let its picture speak of a thousand words,
each one the promise of a lover's creed.
For we belong in this timeless offering,
held between the here and now.

Poem by - Cat @Catkin1973

# POEM 62

Take me where the blue skies sigh
and crystal simmered waters cry.
Where moments are kept for a rainy day,
a memory to chase my sorrow away.
For you are my forever story,
the place where my dreams unfold.
Captured in a tainted heart,
that once was shiny gold.

Poem by - Cat @Catkin1973

# POEM 63

Tides pull me to their depths,
the glistening ocean's call I hear.
Racing, tumbling onto shore,
to kiss my weary steps.
Its darkness is a welcome sight,
cold as stone, black as night.
Still here and now it echoes my cry
and swallows the empty inside.

Poem by - Cat @Catkin1973

# POEM 64

while our words
softly swayed
we sang songs of
sipping lemonade
on a whispered
summer's haze

icy cold and
bittersweet
salty was the
sweat lingering
from the heat,
as the dropping
dripping sunlight
cast over our dancing
into the starry night

Poem by - Michael McCarthy @Free2bmac

# POEM 65

Crystal
Shimmered
Waters gleam,
Upon the Ocean
So serene,
Diamonds in
The sky above,
She whispers
Here, I fall
In love!

Poem by - Anthony Rhead @antsared

# POEM 66

Marvel in the
Glistening,
Oceans call
Whispering,
Sweet melodic
Gentle tunes,
Underneath
Her crescent
Moon..

Poem by - Anthony Rhead @antsared

# POEM 67

summer rain
beneath a midnight
chandelier of stars
wreathing the world
in Otherworldly
light 'n shadows
silver-gleam
ebony mystique
the noir heart blooms
in wild welcome

Poem by - Storm @MadQueenStorm

# POEM 68

A welcomed summer rain pouring down
Stripped her of all her defenses
Her vulnerabilities exposed beneath a midnight chandelier of stars
The beauty of her raw & naked emotions
Not missed by her audience of alone
Tucked away in tender mercies only she can share

Poem by - iAmWriting @AudreySemprun

# POEM 69

clouds dance
dripping sunlight escapes
& suddenly
all the promises
we once
thought broken
challenges us
to share
new dreams
instead

Poem by - George @BklynMercado

# POEM 70

For my thirsty lips
his kiss would be
as welcomed as
summer rain
to the drought

Poem by - Anne @sweetdarkpoetry

# POEM 71

Our love solidified
Two souls became one
Beneath a midnight chandelier of stars
Eternal bliss

Together
A new chapter begins
Our past washed away
A new day
Welcome summer rain

Poem by - Amanda @AmandaJK_

# POEM 72

Afterwards
In the silence
My heart
Grew heavy
With loss
After every moon
Another part of you
Was fading away
While I waned
Upon the ebb
Each lonely day
I weaved a tapestry
Of flowers
From the threads
Of your memory
Now
Countless blossoms
Bloom

Poem by - Ann Bagnall @annieb222
© Ann Bagnall

# POEM 73

In the star infused
Crystal shimmered waters
Of the night
I am drifting
In the silken cascades
Of shoreless rivers
Here in the darkness
As alone as the sea
Time flows unseen
Caught in the current
I disappear
Into the deep pool
Of dreams

Poem by - Ann Bagnall @annieb222
© Ann Bagnall

# POEM 74

I welcome Summer rain
under a midnight chandelier of stars
Teardrop crystals of astral light fall softly,
beckoning me to where you are
Moonlit candles, hung across
a darkened sky
weep gently
extinguished
with broken hearts and last goodbyes

Poem by - Merry Maiden @QueenofCups99

# POEM 75

The glistening ocean's call
A haunting siren song
Disguising her depths
Her secrets and shadows
Into which you can never see
Like brief intervals of a dream
Or bright butterflies drifting by
Delicately unreachable
As the earth is to the sky

Poem by - Ann Bagnall @annieb222
© Ann Bagnall

## POEM 76

A breeze off the Gulf of Mexico
Carries the scent of your sun-kissed skin
Instant nostalgia
Déjà vu
Sunlight dripping down the waves of blue
Tucked Forever away
For these views of you…

The summer has just begun
Starring:
Me.
You.
The Sun.

Poem by - яов @HangryPoet197

# POEM 77

A rhapsody of meteor showers
A tapestry of flowers
The moon rising from the glistening ocean
I sit for hours drowning completely in each sweet moment

I can see the entire cosmos in your eyes tonight ...

Poem by - яов @HangryPoet197

# POEM 78

Beneath a midnight chandelier of stars
the night belonged to us
we were so young and welcomed the summer rain
as we treed stories of wild sky mysteries
that universe our surroundings
two luminous silhouettes... pirouetting

Poem by - Kimberly @bionicanadian

# POEM 79

Beneath a midnight chandelier of stars,
ache for your name,
as I was searching sky for moon,
came welcomed summer rain.

Poem by - Bliss @Bliss_Missed

# POEM 80

A tear
a raindrop
a river
an ocean

Miraculous chemistry
flowing & rolling
Shallow a tear
laughing at your hurt

Deep as the Rhône
beneath a midnight
chandelier of stars

Star-crossed lovers
tethered to celestial orbs
shed raindrop tears
as welcomed summer rain

Poem by - kaleidopathic @kaleidopathic

# POEM 81

Blossom
Welcomed
Summer rain
Upon the
Edge of dry,
World it
Breathed
Relief,
Flowers
Welcomed
Sigh..

Poem by - Anthony Rhead @antsared

# POEM 82

Beneath a midnight
Chandelier of stars,
We expose our deepest scars.
We are together silently sad,
Welcoming back Summer rain;
To hide each category of our brain;
Screaming without sound
This unsustainable chest pain' sun.

Poem by - Lara Reis | Poetry @relaroca

# POEM 83

Strong morning coffee
Butter croissant
Macarons in the afternoon
Sweet treat
Art gallery museum
Sun in Paris warm caress
A walk by the Seine
So romantic
Night brings the shade
Beneath a midnight chandelier
Of stars
Welcomed summer rain
your touch my surrender

Poem by - Just M... @Mjustthat

# POEM 84

Maybe
they may
See, little bit
lonely me,
Here I think
I'm full,
Glistening
Oceans call..

Poem by - Anthony Rhead @antsared

# POEM 85

When the day came
we welcomed
that summer rain
hand holding walks
kiss interrupted talks
flowing rain upon the panes
steamy surround
pleasures abound
hidden underneath
our own little rain cloud.

Poem by - Jaime @JamSt1977

# POEM 86

This gentle end bewitches us,
as the scent of warm lavender fills the night.
It's heady perfume teases us,
as we're lulled beyond impassioned skies.
Love me, let our hearts be free,
as we writhe beneath this midnight chandelier.

Poem by - Cat @Catkin1973

# POEM 87

after a long awaited, eagerly
welcomed summer rain,
the cool night zephyr
explores with her,
tracing the path of her destiny
running imaginary fingers
over shapeshifting clouds
playing a game of dare with fate
beneath a midnight chandelier of stars

Poem by - Pallavi @pallavi31

# POEM 88

Too many boring hours,
eyes bleeding from staring at the sun.
Blistered skin, sandy feet,
irritants of every sense.
Vacations from this friend, that friend,
every friend, miles apart.

None of that matters beneath a midnight chandelier of stars.

Poem by - Jay Heltzer - Writer @JayHeltzer

# POEM 89

We fell in love
Laughed
Fought
Made up
Made love
Jumped thru
Hoops of fire
To be together
Volatile & erratic
A burnt out candle
Dripping wax
Of passion
Cooling as
Welcome
Summer
Rain

Poem by - Silent Echo @Silentecho64

# POEM 90

silver veiled clouds
drift across the night's eyes
fracturing cascades of starlight
into a luminous mosaic
of diffuse dreams
the slumbering sky
now nocturne's canvas
breathlessly awaiting
the soft gold strokes of dawn

Poem by - Storm @MadQueenStorm

# POEM 91

Brook Benton mentioned it; A Rainy Night In Georgia!

But we welcomed the summer rain, is that normal?

But a little bit lonely as raindrops tap the windowpane.

Fogging the glass; harassment? like the Lake
I'm Placid ignoring the pain!

Poem by - OMANXL1 @OMANXL1

# POEM 92

The glistening ocean's call
beckoning the broken-hearted
to seek shoreline

Take refuge
in a tapestry
of rose woven hair
mirrored on crystal
shimmered waters

Her beauty
a collective metaphor
of memories so beautiful
too agonizing to reflect

Poem by - kaleidopathic @kaleidopathic

# POEM 93

Were I to let go of all of my fantasies
I'd miss a mosaic of dreams
that I've painted on my midnight sky
Within the cascades of starlight
abide a myriad of constellations
Shimmering in variants of blues
All pointing me back to you
my summer love

Poem by - iAmWriting @AudreySemprun

# POEM 94

My Cold pale
skin glows
Seductively
Within cascades
Of starlight
& a full bright
moon

Laying flat & stiff
I still seduce

As I remain
A mosaic of
Dreams unfulfilled
Even through
death

Poem by - @femfict

# POEM 95

Within cascades of starlight
Elysian Goddess
absorbs lost souls' sorrows
fusing them into
a mosaic of dreams
summer night's fires
fuel cosmic forges
creating art from pain
finished pieces
sent to Earth
hopeful shooting stars
that never miss
world-weary hearts

Poem by - Jamie Kovalsky @ThePuckishPen

# POEM 96

we missed our chance
too much hurt
to push thru

but we welcomed
the summer rain

it carried our spirits
to a place
where the ink
was so purple
even the sky dissolved

stripped of everything
but passion & warmth

we could heal the pain
& lose ourselves
& melt in that rain

Poem by - Daniel Cummings @DanielC55186873

# POEM 97

though they be dripping sunlight
they are false friends
smiling backward
willing to mire you
in your mistakes

echoes of self
already cut loose
and cast off

let them chase your shadows

look for the friendly hand
that wants to pull you
into the light

Poem by - Daniel Cummings @DanielC55186873

# POEM 98

In a mosaic of dreams
I saw a shadow
l let it be defined
as the darkness in me

Not the moonlight
casting my image
on the cemetery wall

Grief a contextual shift
Loss, fog that doesn't lift
until it is time to see shadows
as the light from the moon
within cascades of starlight

Poem by - kaleidopathic @kaleidopathic

# POEM 99

Venus & Mars
Beneath a midnight chandelier of stars
I commandeered
your heart
Chapters of rapture
Passion as an Art

Connections made deeper than carnal bliss

It's the way I'm tasting
home in your kiss
It's the way you make me
whole from the broken bits

Poem by - яов @HangryPoet197

# POEM 100

Welcomed summer rain
beading off your skin
Bring me into your depths
until we're too out of breath
to swim

Midnight brontides
Perhaps distant thunder
But none of it matches your wonder

Love is awake.

Gravity grows stronger...

Poem by - яов @HangryPoet197

# POEM 101

All the broken pieces,
the jagged sharp edges,
a mosaic of dreams.
Each shard catches on the moon you hung for me,
and within cascades of starlight,
the ultimate mystery,
in the darkest of the night,
what looks doesn't see.

Poem by - Bliss @Bliss_Missed

# POEM 102

We expected grandma's word-bless,
Each midsummer besides last year.

Below this artificial mosaic of dreams;
Which falls into a cascade of gleams.
The phone is quiet again this feast.

She won't be here, my dear,
Pamper each one with invest
From her deepest regal heart's chest.

Poem by - Lara Reis | Poetry @relaroca

# POEM 103

Summer love
Passed me by;
Soft rain dripped
Down tearstained skies.
Blue dreams curled
On warm night sand;
Broken seashells
Slipped through my hands.
Waves of hope
Crashed and faded—
Sunshine romance,
So overrated.

Poem by - Pawla @lightm0tifs

# POEM 104

This heat burns like fire
as it flickers at the heart of me.
Fuelled by sweet devotion
from an endless teasing kiss.
For you are my passion,
the kindling for my flame.
So thankful to be coveted
by this welcomed summer rain.

Poem by - Cat @Catkin1973

# POEM 105

### A Mosaic of Dreams

The amber ones, filled with tears.
Turquoise reminds me of my uncle's swap meet jewelry.
Yellow meals,
green dragon flights,
red #ghosts dancing awkwardly.
Azure moments of isolation,
and one brown tile, the one that got away.

Poem by - Jay Heltzer - Writer @JayHeltzer

# POEM 106

before me
the mosaic of dreams
captures
not only the shadows
of my life
but those rainbows
I once thought
I misplaced
but were hiding
in my heart
the whole time

Poem by - George @BklynMercado

# POEM 107

Memories of departed souls
fall within cascades of starlight
Mosaic dreams bring them back to us
on brilliant shimmering nights

Poem by - Merry Maiden @QueenofCups99

# POEM 108

Within cascades of starlight
My midnight fantasies fall
Caught by you

Together we're a mosaic of dreams
An epic tale waiting to be told

There's poetry
In the way you move
An unwritten story
Begging to be told by my touch

We'll inscribe our desires
On each other's bodies

Poem by - DK Marie Romance Author @DKMarieAuthor

# POEM 109 AND 110

Dreamboats whisper in
Tropical oasis, the
Dancing Light of dawn.

~

Dripping sunlight stain
Calm reflection of islets,
Tree glow to rhythm.

Poems by @SerlinaRose767

# POEM 111 AND 112

Dripping sunlight
Beaming bright
Dazzling sight
Senses excite
Such delight

~

Completing
A mosaic of dreams
Under his moonbeams
Night by night
Lucid and bright

Poems by - Grace @Ainneamhag

# POEM 113

hazy summer sky
refracting crystal
shimmered waters
splinter aloft,
drenching paved
paths and
park benches

Poem by - Michael McCarthy @Free2bmac

# POEM 114

Splender summer
sunset upon
the glistening
ocean's call
swells crest
and crash
safer we remain
below it all

Poem by - Michael McCarthy @Free2bmac

# POEM 115

Late at night as
somnolence slowly
asserts its superiority
we talk, we plan, we hope.
Starlight cascades upon our
mosaic of dreams,
it's blessing necessary
to furnish future with sparkle,
and it's dreamers with desire

Poem by - COMPOSED @21composed

# POEM 116

thorns pricking
fingers weaving this
tapestry of flowers
vines and stems
we tied into heart
shaped knots

watching shooting
stars from the
back of my truck
laying out on a bed
of forget me nots

Poem by - Michael McCarthy @Free2bmac

# POEM 117

Mosaic of dreams within,
cascades of starlight
summers reflections
compass my direction
guide me to the wonders of sky
beyond the veiled waterfall
where stars run counterclockwise
the future is the past,
summering into a thousand
yesterdays
the forest sorrowful

Poem by - Kimberly @bionicanadian

# POEM 118

I chose each one especially
Dressed in my yearnings
The better parts of you
For i always longed
Of happy ever afters
Escaping into a mosaic of dreams
Don't shatter my illusion
Sweet sky of darkening calm
Within cascades of starlight
You become the better man

Poem by - Just M... @Mjustthat

# POEM 119

My mind all a shiver
As I sit down by the river
Beside crystal shimmered
Waters that are glimmered
Reflecting myself back at me
That lonesome guy I see
Memories sliding in time
A sad poetic rhyme
Of forgotten summer days
Locked away in a mindful daze

Poem by - T.J. Hübner Writing - Poet & Author @hubner_t

# POEM 120

I try to piece together
This intricate mosaic of dreams
The endings always hidden
Their beginnings I never see
I raise my hands to moonlit skies
And ask her what she means
I beg for her to take away
An unending cycle of endless dream

Poem by - Cat @Catkin1973

# POEM 121

Those fiery thoughts
That kept you awake,
Within cascades of starlight,
Set your dreams ablaze.
They no longer count
They have ceased to be
Like a distant sunset
An autumn leaf.
All that matters now
Is what you did,
What you've never undone
And the pain you feel.

Poem by - Jill Webb Words @jillwebbwords

# POEM 122

Make a wish and let it fly
Beyond the view of endless sky
Whisper not his name
For silence is the only way
Picture him inside your mind
Within cascades of starlight shine
Never let the image fade
For wishes end with the break of day

Poem by - Cat @Catkin1973

# POEM 123

Humanity
Just a blink of an eye

Who else but
Has sense to see
Cascades of starlight
Or a mosaic of dreams

Alas I wish
We would have learned our lesson
But maybe our brains are still to little
To act by reason

Poem by - Peer @ViewfinderPM

# POEM 124

the dancing light of dawn
banishes the shadows of night

flowers in meadows are abloom
and smiling to the summer sun

like them, i dance and sing
bearing an ocean deep sorrow in my mind

for summer will return the next year
there is no promise of me being here

Poem by - Bithi Paul @BithiPaulAuthor

# POEM 125

drawn to follow
where the journey goes
I walk through
vignette by vignette
an odd mosaic
of dreams
just bits I remember
in the waking world
yet, their potency
not decomposed
I feel like I'm living
between the whispers
of those other worlds

Poem by - Dee Lusk @hsdee

## POEM 126

i dance in the meadow
to the orchestra of crickets
beneath a midnight
chandelier of stars

i come out of my trance
the sweltering heat wins

drops of water falls
on my upturned face

with arms wide open
i welcome the summer rain

Poem by - Bithi Paul @BithiPaulAuthor

# POEM 127

weaving a mosaic of dreams
in the stories i write
within cascades of starlight
never to be forgotten

sheets of paper are transient
like bright summer days
my stories will be alive
even after my death

Poem by - Bithi Paul @BithiPaulAuthor

# POEM 128

Come Closer to my heart
This is the place we breathe and part
Her sunsets grasp your hand
Sweet harvests to our land
And You'll find me waiting there
By the willow in the air.

And my face will be brushing...

Against your hair

Poem by - alan sawyer @alternativepen

# POEM 129

Shattered dreams
Made into a mural
On the walls of my mind
Each shard shines
Fractal light
From the hidden sun
Of my soul

Poem by - Rebekah Webb @Story_Tweets

# POEM 130

strawflowers scent the summer light
as morning kisses the sky
dreams awakening open their eyes
as diamonds dance in the flow
of golden breaths blown
the spin and dance
of words between worlds
becomes a melody to sing the day away
a gentle reprieve from night's troubles

Poem by - Storm @MadQueenStorm

# POEM 131

Champagne summers of romantic tunes
light up like ocean blues of forever
as morning kisses the sky
purple dawn of diamonds
dance in the flow to teacup sunrises
sipping radiant morning dew
of different hued... colors

Poem by - Kimberly @bionicanadian

# POEM 132

On a hot summer's day
The glistening ocean's call
Sings out for all to play
With a song to enthral
Inviting bathers to partake
Of its sprawling tidal flow
As it crashes and breaks
Beneath the suns warming glow

Poem by - T.J. Hübner Writing - Poet & Author @hubner_t

# POEM 133

I see you on the horizon
As morning kisses the sky
As fresh as the morning dawning
Kissed by the new day's sun
As diamonds dance in the flow
The ocean's current
Calling me home
Kisses for the morning
Kisses for the night
Kisses upon kisses
To my soul's delight

Poem by - iAmWriting @AudreySemprun

# POEM 134

I lie awake
tossing in
confusion
Until
a mosaic of
dreams
comes to ease
my pain
Old friends from
faraway lands
enter to play
and comfort
I sleep until
dawn
At peace

Poem by - Dark Wolf Writer II More Tales to Tell @dark_backup

# POEM 135

Throwback Thursday? the poetry is retro futuristic.

In a mosaic of dreams I luxuriate!

I live between the whispers / voices in my head.

Embedded in the midst; play by play description? by iPhone, loose leaf, ink or lead!

Poem by - OMANXL1 @OMANXL1

# POEM 136

As diamonds dance in the flow,
the evening lingers, afraid to go.
As moonlight grows faint,
the evening exerts restraint,
fading quickly into paint.
As morning kisses the sky
the evening quietly dies.

Poem by - Alisa @WhimsyCheshire

# POEM 137

As I drift to sleep
my body signals the dreamscape I shall enter.
I may fearfully wrestle with the screaming demons of my soul.
Or I may sway with angelic beings
into the constellation
that is my heart space.

Poem by - Kat @katy_lady_b

# POEM 138

I'll gladly follow you
Leave it all behind
Cold winter storms

For the sunshine & her bloom

For the meadow lark that sings
As the morning kisses the sky

Dawn births a new day

As diamonds dance in the flow
Take me in your loving arms
~Dance with me

Poem by - Just M... @Mjustthat

## POEM 139

As morning kisses the sky,
We share breakfast high;
As diamonds dance in the flow,
We talked about tomorrow.
And a bit about us and the glow
In your eyes and mine.
We smelled as summer kin,
A bit of sand and original sin.

Poem by - Lara Reis | Poetry @relaroca

# POEM 140

A world away from winter
As morning kisses the sky
Eyes speak
A language of love
For there is no other

Our hearts in steady beat
Passion knows no bounds
Sweet scented jasmine
Roses petals on the bed

As diamonds dance in the flow
A summer to remember

Poem by - Just M... @Mjustthat

# POEM 141

I dream in shades of you
Colour that sparkles in the light
Merging with sunbeams
Thoughts as whispers
A delicate caress
I hear them in my sleep
Warming sensual
A summer affair
As morning kisses the sky
As diamonds dance in the flow
You take me to paradise

Poem by - Just M... @Mjustthat

# POEM 142

As morning kisses the sky
Dew drops say goodbye
Birds and bees start to fly
The world gently goes on by
And as I open my eyes
He is there by my side

Poem by - Grace @Ainneamhag

# POEM 143

I lie within a tapestry
of flowers all around
Displayed like a painting
that does astound
An artists imagination
clear & bright
A mosaic of dreams
to bring pure delight
The colours, so vibrant
& reflective of light
From the heavens, we
together bask in sunlight

Poem by - T.J. Hübner Writing - Poet & Author @hubner_t

# POEM 144

As morning
Kisses the sky
The sea aches
With beauty
Sighs and murmurs
Twisted driftwood
Clamour of birdsong
Dawn cascading
Shimmering silken
Blushing rose
In this moment
I feel you near
I am drenched
In gentle colours
A heartbeat short
Of eternity

Poem by - Ann Bagnall @annieb222
© AnnBagnall

# POEM 145

The silent moon
Gently bathes
The sea in silver
Transforming
The lazuline surface
To sparkling black
As diamonds dance in the flow
Weaving the sweet night
With magic and gold
Darkness and whispers
Ever revealing
Ever concealing
Ever out of reach

Poem by - Ann Bagnall @annieb222
© Ann Bagnall

# POEM 146

morning kisses the sky

clouds unveil
a midnight beauty
sand glittering golden
against her skin

diamond spray
of a wounded heron
a shimmering backdrop
to her ocean swells

her contours of love
have eclipsed the sun
& the warmth in her eyes
have tamed this sea

Poem by - Daniel Cummings @DanielC55186873

# POEM 147

In the warmth of
a summer night
Within the cascades
Of starlight
I lie upon the meadows
grassy sheet of green
Looking up at the
twinkling nightly scene
As the waves of awe
sweep me up high
Amongst the heavens
where my soul does dreamily fly

Poem by - T.J. Hübner Writing - Poet & Author @hubner_t

# POEM 148

I live between the whispers
Of my simulating hopes,
between the megillahs
Of my nostalgia.
and between the rumbles
Of my long-lost freedom.

My existence is capricious.
Yet I want to run on a mosaic
Of my squandered dreams,
forgetting my regrets.

Poem by - Kavya Janani. U @UKavyajanani

# POEM 149

Tender is the touch we share
As morning kisses the sky
The darkness is no longer here
Our here and now
Brought to light
The whispers are a silent song
Doubts and fears grow quiet
This is all that matters now
Two hearts
One beat
Forever you and I

Poem by - Cat @Catkin1973

# POEM 150

Lost in thoughts anew
Ones that seem so darkly true
I watch this river slip softly by
Let it wash away the truths that lie
Fill my heart with strength and light
Let this image hold the vision tight
As diamonds dance in the flow
I promise to never let you go

Poem by - Cat @Catkin1973

# POEM 151

I awaken as the morning
kisses the sky
& the stars close their eyes
I awaken as the world
begins to stir
whispering you're alive
I awaken to the blessings
of the dawn
I awaken next to you
& that is enough

Poem by - George @BklynMercado

# POEM 152 AND 153

As morning kisses the sky
I die a little more
without your presence,
without your love

~

The breath of midnight's warmth softly awakens me
intoxicates, entices me,
yet frustrates me as I realize
it's not your arms holding me

Poems by - Anne @sweetdarkpoetry

# POEM 154

Stelliferous precipitation
Liquid diamond libations
Frappuccino frames freeze
These days I'm awake in-between
I'm cultivating a mosaic of dreams
To match your kaleidoscope eyes.
Your body
has not a single tan line
That I can find
Summer sand sublime

Poem by - яов @HangryPoet197

# POEM 155

I have to leave
As the morning kisses the sky
But
I return every night

Like the breeze
Which brings calm onto your skin
After the heat of the day

Poem by - Peer @ViewfinderPM

# POEM 156

As morning kisses the sky
dawn & I rise blushing pink;
emotions clad purpleblack
luxurious deepnight skin;
sleepsoft eyes smile -- sated sigh
Each sunrise I build a bridge --
soulsung words between our worlds
Reality is defined for me
in this bubble of certainty

Poem by - Mamathi Style @CMamathi

# POEM 157

Cusp between monsoon & summer
Magic days, will of nature. As
seasons slipped into the other
they were not alone this change

In a whispered summer haze
of rain-laden golden-greys
everything us shifted seam
Still feels unreal, as though a dream

Poem by - Mamathi Style @CMamathi

# POEM 158

As Morning Kisses The Sky
I kiss your forehead
As Diamonds Dance In The Flow
My eyes smile like a pearl's glow
I often wonder
As I hold you my precious doll
If there was ever unending love
Then it's here until eternity!

Poem by - Sangeeta @smusicj68

# POEM 159

i long to see the ocean
but she is so far

in the sound of crystal shimmered
waters of rain i hear
the glistening ocean's call

behind a tapestry of flowers
i lie in the meadow of summer
while rain drenches my body
a mermaid of dry land

Poem by - Bithi Paul @BithiPaulAuthor

# POEM 160

Tickled pink moon
drawn to a heavenly romance
as morning kisses the sky
uniting nature's seductive feminine palate

Sunlight dances on branches
as sky bows down
to her ravishing blossoms
& culminate in an explosion of color

Tickling winds tease
an eruption
of little petal tears

Poem by - kaleidopathic @kaleidopathic

# POEM 161

my withering spirit revives
as morning kisses the sky
and diamonds dance
in the flow of sunlight

i go to the riverside
and jump into the water

i swim with the swans
and fishes tickle my toes

the scorching sun smiles, asking
isn't it good to be alive

Poem by - Bithi Paul @BithiPaulAuthor

# POEM 162

a summer's season of love
remembered with tender regret
when the breath of midnight warmth
gently brushes across untouched skin
the heart trembles and sighs
oh those distant days now gone
wishing they could be relived

Poem by - Storm @MadQueenStorm

# POEM 163

Summer — the Season for love
Love — the reason for summer
Come dance with me in the rain
To the beat of our very own drummer.

I'll stare at you in your eyes.
Lose myself there for a while —
Seas aren't as massive nor deep
Nor have they that beautiful smile.

Poem by - Ben @BenjaminDStone

# POEM 164

The currents
Of our passion
Tender like water
Engulf everything
Rivers flow unseen
The breath of midnight warmth
As sweet as a petal
Blooming
In our secret garden
Unfurling
Spilling over
As the moon-shadows deepen
In the fragrant pool
Of desire

Poem by - Ann Bagnall @annieb222
©Ann Bagnall

# POEM 165

Shadows grow long
A summer's season of love
Slowly dying
Under empty skies
Raindrops on jasmine
Crescendo of rain
Petals weep fragrance
Night aching
Under star sprinkled oceans
And I surrender
To the moment
Like a raindrop
Returned to the stream

Poem by - Ann Bagnall @annieb222
© Ann Bagnall

# POEM 166

My place of peace will always be the ocean
My house by the beach my secret getaway
Now I share it happily
A summer's season of love
Nights of heat and passion
The breath of midnight warmth
Together
Our future, an unknown path I couldn't wait to travel

Poem by - Amanda @AmandaJK_

# POEM 167

The breath of midnight warmth technology
Keeps U ever on my mind
All my circuits shorting out
Sending gamma rays into the cosmos
A summer's season of love
Never to B forgotten
Searching into the atmosphere
For traces of the light
That leads me back 2U

Poem by - iAmWriting @AudreySemprun

## POEM 168

the field had become
something greater
than a tapestry of flowers
now a field of rainbows
waiting to be held
& dreams
dying to be born

Poem by - George @BklynMercado

## POEM 169

The breath of midnight jazz
nocturnal rhythmic brass
by dreamers full of class
soulful songs of cities & lovers

A summer's season song of love
she's tall & walks so fine
she sang it smoothly line by line
he sang it in Portuguese sublime
of a girl so lovely

Poem by - kaleidopathic @kaleidopathic

## POEM 170

With you, it had just begun.
Your summer's season love.
She breathes midnight warmth.
Around your skin goosebump.
As you assess on her after the sun.
Caressing her fair complexion,
You chase that lass affection.
Hun, just don't.

Poem by - Lara Reis | Poetry @relaroca

# POEM 171

A summer season of love
Memories rest comfortably
At the side of a quiet lake
The sun baking the sand
And a gentle breeze
Softly warms her hair
The breath of midnight warmth
Lulls her back to sleep
Where she can rest
At their quiet lake
Once again
Soaking in the dream
Of together

Poem by - iAmWriting @AudreySemprun

# POEM 172

One candle
for each day
I try
Windows
Stairs
Tables
and chairs
Even mountains
won't suffice
Peridot flames dance eternal
Diamond heart breaks apart
As morning kisses the sky
I feel
your lips touch mine
And I know
One candle
for each day
I shall burn
for you

Poem by - Mirai Amell @AmellMirai

# POEM 173

The breath of midnight warmth,
and how it speaks your name,
a summer's season of love,
I'll never be the same.
Can't quite figure out,
where you end and I begin,
entwined in grand illusion,
or a secret sin.

Poem by - Bliss @Bliss_Missed

# POEM 174

### A Summer's Season of Love

E was cute, but aloof.
A and I knew it wouldn't work, but when
she sang, it worked on me.
R wanted more, much, much more.
F locked my heart for good,
even when S worked her way inside.

So much love in one season, over and over.

Poem by - Jay Heltzer - Writer @JayHeltzer

## POEM 175

I dream a dream
Of trickling streams,
Babbling brooks
And fish on hooks
Playfully returned free
To swim again carefree
Then
I wish upon a star
To hide the scars
Of humanities neglect
In still waters that reflect
The welcomed summer rain
To wash away nature's pain

Poem by - T.J. Hübner Writing - Poet & Author @hubner_t

# POEM 176

We stood
motionless
our bodies caressed
by the ardour
of satin hands

we tilted our chins
and opened wide our mouths
thirsting for the salvation
falling fast from the sky

a blessed renewal
with such sweet relief
we welcomed the kiss
of summer rain

Poem by - Andrea @RainyDayRibbons

# POEM 177 AND 178

Morning awoke in ripples
stretched a wide blue veil
over crystal shimmered waters
sleek seabirds arose
curved against the grain of light
a tapestry of feathered flowers
responding to the glistening oceans call

~

Breathless
we stretch out our souls
beneath a midnight chandelier of stars

Poems by - Andrea @RainyDayRibbons

# POEM 179

The morning after
I wear the ghosts of your love
like a whispered summer haze

a breath of gold
trickling along my skin
a river of pleasure
connecting every freckle

mellifluous, my heart sings
shaming the nightingale
dripping sunlight from every note

Poem by - Andrea @RainyDayRibbons

# POEM 180

More than
A summers season
Of love

It's every reason
From the
Cosmos up above

That this
Is the start of

Our
Instant
Eternal
Love...

Poem by - Grace @Ainneamhag

# POEM 181

Amongst the darkest of nights
Can be seen, such pure delights
A heavenly nocturnal sight
Illuminated by moonlight
For beneath a midnight
Chandelier of stars dancing in flight
As if the skies did colourfully ignite
Is nature's own aurora of light

Poem by - T.J. Hübner Writing - Poet & Author @hubner_t

# POEM 182

High summer
the meadows abloom
kaleidoscopic splashes
vying for attention
an intensity of colour

but he
he only has eyes
for her gentle grace
and the way her hair
ripples with gold
in the dancing light of dawn

Poem by - Andrea @RainyDayRibbons

# POEM 183

Every night they dance

Dreams painted
with the breath
of midnight warmth

Souls bound
by wistful sighs
and yesterday's lace

Fragile hearts
butterflies
of memories wings

Eternal ghosts
floating thru
passages of time

Only to fade
as morning
kisses the sky

Poem by - Coffee & Lyrics @livezformusic

# POEM 184

Against the sky
a fading flight
of indigo swallows
tail streamers
dissolving
to fragments of grey
gone too soon
like a summer season of love
tethered eternally
to the phases of the moon

Poem by - Andrea @RainyDayRibbons

# POEM 185

Pulled from sleep
my mind's eye
still rich with dreaming
a breath of midnight warmth
still scattered on my skin
losing my hold
on these ephemeral pieces of you

Poem by - Andrea @RainyDayRibbons

# POEM 186

As morning kisses
the sky above
Questions are asked
of our true love

Was it simply just
a summer romance
Or are,
Our hearts locked
in a soulful trance

Eye to eye, as diamonds
dance in the flow
Of a youthful love
in a fresh new glow

Now a togetherness of one

Poem by - T.J. Hübner Writing - Poet & Author @hubner_t

# POEM 187 AND 188

Await a summer's season,
Of love inducing dreaming,
Of walks along the shore,
Hand in hand, stood before..

~

The breath of midnight warmth,
Emanating touch, affection through
The veins, feathers on the shore

Poems by - Anthony Rhead @antsared

# POEM 189

Neon lights
bathing your bare back

Vials of lavender
the promises in my mouth

Your hands are time
melting icicles

My body
the longest summer
season of love
a breath of midnight warmth
on a cold French window

Let me live as your last kiss
I refuse to die a wound

Poem by - Sakshi Narula @mssakshinarula

# POEM 190

Is this only a summer's season of love
Where they held each other close amongst the dunes
Where tides crept their way upon its barren sands
And left lost trails of treasures for lovers then to find
Remembered kisses to heal a heart once found beyond goodbye

Poem by - Cat @Catkin1973

# POEM 191

Golden clouds
Ephemeral dreams
Topaz summer
Fleeting and fleeing
Castles wash away
in turquoise desire
Our footsteps
etched in pink sand
Love is in silence
in every heartbeat
in every breath
For
You and me
stay
frozen forever
In that midnight warmth

Poem by - Mirai Amell @AmellMirai

# POEM 192

Gentle in sleep he moves me
His beauty is mine alone
I see the things they do not see
Tender is the man I know
His breath of midnight warmth
Is the movement in my hair
Soft now, his tenderness lingers
Unknown to him
But always there....

Poem by - Cat @Catkin1973

# POEM 193

In a blanket, wrapped
watching the world
from a window seat
heavy words in my mind

until your voice
soft against my senses
calls me back to bed
and all at once
my heart is home
snuggled safe
against your side

you bring me to life
as morning kisses the sky

Poem by - Andrea @RainyDayRibbons

## POEM 194

it was
the last dance
after a summer's season
of love
where the first kiss
of fall aproached
teasing me
like a old lover
whispering
that the time
for my summer fling
was over
it was time
to come home

Poem by - George @BklynMercado

# POEM 195

#InstantEternal YES
A summer's season of love
floats on the breath of.. midnight warmth
your quick smile catches me off guard
invokes a smile from where words are quiet
but this time the daffodil's sonnet
of moon filled words
tumbles from onyx skies
you are who my heart.. loves

Poem by - Kimberly @bionicanadian

# POEM 196

Summer's season of love,
I will be a light in your night,
when the wind is blowing I will be your warmth,
when you begin to fall I will be your angel and carry you,
when you run out of words I will be your poetry,
when you hurt I will love you forever

Poem by - Gail Pilkington @Lilly2Rose3

# POEM 197

A mosaic of dreams
Stitched together
With gossamer thread
Filled with intrepid hope
Encompassing starlight
Comprised of wishes
Shimmering incandescence
Illuminating revelations
Hidden in the clouds

Poem by - WickedSkullFate @FortunatusL

# POEM 198

bees hover over the flowers
as the sun kisses them
brightening nature with
a summer's season of love

the warm breath of midnight is soothing
after the suffocating heat of the day

the scent of jasmine fills the air
and lulls me to sleep's rainbow dreams

Poem by - Bithi Paul @BithiPaulAuthor

# POEM 199

Exhaled the breath
Of midnight, warmth,
Summers balmy air,
On horizon outline,
Adventure bound a
Ship somewhere

Poem by - Anthony Rhead @antsared

# POEM 200

A summer's season of love
Sweet the apple blossom
Joy of my heart
Green fields of the meadow

As night descends
eiderdown soft comfort

Dreams are dancing
Cheek to cheek
Gentle hands gentle kisses
Where now begins

The breath of midnight warmth

Poem by - Just M... @Mjustthat

# POEM 201

A night owl breathing the breath of midnight warmth.

Relieving tension the anxiety / apprehension that swarms.

It's trying to build a memorial in my aura!

I didn't yield, didn't swoon in this Aquarius Full Moon; a better tomorrow?

Poem by - OMANXL1 @OMANXL1

# POEM 202

The breath of
midnight warmth
caresses damp
skin in
anticipation
of passionate
love
Dawn comes
We rest in blissful
slumber

Poem by - Dark Wolf Writer II More Tales to Tell @dark_backup

# POEM 203

We stood and gazed
Upon the silks of darkness
That draped across the winter sky.
We found peace
Beneath
A midnight chandelier of stars

Underneath
The glow from the moon,
With the bitter air and
Blinding snow too.
It's here that
I fell in love with
You

Because in this place
Of darkness and light
We knew exactly
Where we wanted to be…
Together…
Always and forever.

Poem by - Elizabeth Harper @eharperpoetry

# POEM 204

Old dusty blinds are
Dripping sunlight into
Sad, tired eyes

Awakening the sorrow
Of starting another day
In the same old life

Because being blessed
Of waking up in the world today
Meaning sacrificing everything

Just so the bills get paid.

Poem by - Elizabeth Harper @eharperpoetry

## POEM 205

When the absence
Of your warm embrace
Made my cold heart ache

My eyes swelled until tears fell.

Now a tapestry of flowers
Hangs in each room

To replace the scent of you.

Poem by - Elizabeth Harper @eharperpoetry

# POEM 206

A summers season of love was coming to a close
I was just wanting something deep enough
that had a chance to grow
The breath of midnight warmth
Bled off the edges
of the eye of a storm
With awe, thundering
Fall was coming
Soon, this all will be nothing

Poem by - яов @HangryPoet197

# POEM 207

Your eyes adorned with little sprites
As daylight fades on the edge of night
Bliss is
Laying beneath the Perseids
demanding wishes
This is everything splendid

As sunlight kisses the morning sky
I notice that brewing storm in you eyes

Soon you'll Fall away

Poem by - яов @HangryPoet197

# POEM 208

Lyrical on the inside,
As diamonds dance in the flow
We fly,
Born on the wind of fire
To a thousand fervent beats
Of each other's
Thirsts,
For we are the whispers
Between dreams
Sighed within
The breath of midnight warmth

Joint poem by - Dawn Serbert @atreya2112
and Stuart Matthews @the_allot_ment

www.ingramcontent.com/pod-product-compliance
Lightning Source LLC
Chambersburg PA
CBHW070630220526
45466CB00001B/138